STEP-BY-STEP

Puddings & Desserts

STEP-BY-STEP

Puddings & Desserts

CARA HOBDAY

||| •PARRAGON• |||

First published in Great Britain in 1995 by
Parragon Book Service Ltd
Unit 13–17
Avonbridge Trading Estate
Atlantic Road
Avonmouth
Bristol BS11 9QD

ISBN 1-85813-899-X (hbk)
ISBN 0-75251-252-8 (pbk)

Produced by Haldane Mason, London

Printed in Italy

Acknowledgements:

Art Direction: Ron Samuels
Editor: Joanna Swinnerton
Series Design: Pedro & Frances Prá-Lopez/Kingfisher Design
Page Design: Somewhere Creative
Photography: Iain Bagwell
Styling: Rachel Jukes
Home Economist: Cara Hobday

Photographs on pages 6, 20, 34, 48 and 62 are reproduced by permission of
ZEFA Picture Library UK Ltd.

Note:
Cup measurements in this book are for American cups. Tablespoons are assumed to be 15 ml.
Unless otherwise stated, milk is assumed to be full-fat, eggs are standard size 2 and pepper is
freshly ground black pepper.

Contents

CHAPTER ONE

Quick & Easy

You may find yourself in a situation where a dessert needs to be rustled up in a hurry – for unexpected guests, family meals, or hungry teenagers – and that is when you turn to this section! Here are six versions of wonderful puddings that are ready in no time.

A well-stocked store cupboard makes it easier to put last-minute creations together – stock up on brandysnaps, ratafia biscuits (cookies) or macaroons, Madeira (pound) cake, sponge fingers (lady-fingers), eggs, longlife cream, canned fruit, raisins, dried fruit, golden (light corn) syrup and canned custard.

A quick dessert can be made by baking fruit – try apples, pears or figs, drizzled with a little honey – or simply combine fruit with cream and custard for a quick fruit fool. Some canned fruits make excellent alternatives to fresh, especially if you are cooking or baking. I never hesitate to use canned blackcurrants, apricots, raspberries or mangoes.

Opposite: *With a little imagination a delicious pudding can often be made in very little time from the most basic ingredients.*

STEP 1

STEP 2

STEP 3

STEP 5

CHERRY CLAFOUTIS

This is a hot dessert that is simple and quick to put together. Try the batter with other seasonal or canned fruits. Apricots and plums are particularly delicious.

SERVES 6

125 g/4 oz/1 cup plain (all-purpose) flour
4 eggs, lightly beaten
2 tbsp caster (superfine) sugar
pinch of salt
600 ml/1 pint/2½ cups milk
butter for greasing
500 g/1 lb black cherries, fresh or canned,
    stoned (pitted)
3 tbsp brandy
1 tbsp sugar to decorate

1 Sift the flour into a large bowl. Make a well in the centre and add the eggs, sugar and salt.

2 Draw in the flour and whisk.

3 Add the milk and whisk until smooth.

4 Butter a 1.75 litre/3 pint/3½ cup ovenproof serving dish and pour in half of the batter.

5 Spoon over the cherries and pour the remaining batter over the top. Sprinkle the brandy over the batter.

6 Bake in a preheated oven at 180°C/350°F/Gas Mark 4 for 40 minutes.

7 Remove from the oven and just before serving sprinkle over the sugar. Serve warm, from the dish.

STEP 1

STEP 2

STEP 3

STEP 7

SCOTCH MIST

In our family, crannachan, as it is more commonly known, has always been called Scotch Mist, and now I know the origin of it – good Scotch whisky! This is a wholesome dish, which improves if left overnight.

SERVES 4–6

500 g/1 lb/generous 3 cups raspberries,
    fresh or frozen
3 tbsp Scotch whisky
300 ml/½ pint/1¼ cups double (heavy)
    cream
4 tbsp heather honey (if not available, use
    clear honey)
60 g/2 oz/⅓ cup oatmeal

1 Reserve 175 g/6 oz/scant 1 cup of the raspberries and put the rest into a bowl with the Scotch whisky. Set aside.

2 Whip the cream until softly stiff.

3 Stir in the honey and oatmeal. If the cream turns soft, whip again until stiff.

4 Spoon a few raspberries into the bottom of each serving glass, or spoon half the raspberries into the bottom of a large glass bowl.

5 Spoon half the cream mixture over the raspberries, then add the remaining raspberries.

6 Spoon the remaining cream over the top. Chill for at least 1 hour, preferably overnight.

7 Mash the reserved raspberries with a wooden spoon, or blend them in a blender or food processor. Press them through a sieve (strainer).

8 When ready to serve, pour a little of the sieved (strained) raspberries over each glass or over the whole bowl.

OATMEAL

Although there are different types of oatmeal available, they are all made from the same thing; the only difference is how much the oats have been milled. I always use the medium-cut one that still has some fine, floury content, as opposed to the slightly more gritty version with no 'dust'.

CREPES SUZETTE

They don't come much more French than this one! This classic dessert is served in restaurants everywhere.

STEP 1

STEP 4

STEP 5

STEP 6

SERVES 4–6

125 g/4 oz/1 cup plain (all-purpose) flour
1 egg
1 egg yolk
300 ml/¹/₂ pint/1¹/₄ cups milk
60 g/2 oz/¹/₄ cup butter, melted
grated rind of 1 orange
250 g/8 oz/1 cup granulated sugar
150 ml/¹/₄ pint/²/₃ cup water
pared rind of 1 orange
melted butter, for frying
juice of 1 orange
250 ml/8 fl oz/1 cup orange-flavoured
    liqueur
1 orange, peeled and segmented

1 Sift the flour into a bowl and make a well in the centre. Add the egg, egg yolk, milk and butter, and draw in the flour. Whisk to a smooth batter. Stir in the orange rind.

2 Leave the pancake batter to rest for 30 minutes.

3 Put the sugar and water into a saucepan and bring to a gentle boil. Add the orange rind and cook gently until the syrup coats the back of a spoon, about 5 minutes. Set aside.

4 Meanwhile, brush a frying pan (skillet) or pancake pan with a little melted butter and place over a medium heat. Tilt the pan (skillet) to one side and pour in about 50 ml/2 fl oz/¹/₄ cup of the batter. Tilt the pan in the opposite direction immediately, so that the whole base is covered in batter.

5 After about 1 minute, or when the pancake is dry on top, toss it and cook the other side for another minute. Make 8–12 pancakes and keep warm in a low oven. Place 2 pancakes on each warmed serving plate, either flat or folded.

6 Reheat the syrup and stir in the orange juice, 150 ml/¹/₄ pint/²/₃ cup of the liqueur and the segmented orange. Pour a little over each serving plate.

7 Heat the remaining liqueur gently in a small pouring pan. It may ignite itself, but if it does not, set a lighted match to it and pour over the pancakes immediately. This is most effective if done at the serving table. You can warm the liqueur gently in the kitchen, take it to the table and ignite it. Blow out the flames immediately.

CHOCOLATE COCONUT LAYER

This is a rich, easy dessert for chocolate-lovers. If you can't wait, it can be eaten straightaway, still warm and gooey, or it can be chilled until set and served with coffee.

STEP 1

SERVES 6–8

200 g/7 oz/7 squares dark chocolate, broken into pieces
300 g/10 oz/1¼ cups full-fat soft cheese
60 g/2 oz/⅔ cup grated or desiccated (shredded) coconut
250 g/8 oz/2 cups digestive biscuits (graham crackers), crumbled

TO DECORATE:
icing (confectioners') sugar
coconut curls or desiccated (shredded) coconut

1 Melt the chocolate in a heatproof bowl set over a saucepan of barely simmering water for 10 minutes. Do not let the water splash into the bowl, as it will affect the texture of the chocolate.

2 Turn off the heat. Add the soft cheese to the chocolate and stir till well blended and smooth.

3 Stir in the grated or desiccated (shredded) coconut.

4 Place half of the biscuit (cracker) crumbs on the bottom of a shallow 1.1 litre/2 pint/4½ cup dish.

5 Layer with half the chocolate mixture, then another layer of the remaining biscuit (cracker) crumbs, finishing with a layer of the remaining chocolate mixture. Chill for 2 hours.

6 Dust with icing (confectioners') sugar and coconut curls or desiccated (shredded) coconut before serving.

STEP 2

COCONUT CURLS

If using a fresh coconut, drain the milk and split the coconut apart using a hammer. Remove the flesh from the shell in large pieces. To make the curls, peel down one side of each piece of coconut flesh with a peeler and use the resulting curls for decoration.

STEP 3

TIPS

This can be kept for up to 5 days in the refrigerator but remember to cover the dish carefully so that the dessert doesn't absorb other flavours.

If you prefer, you can make individual desserts using 6–8 ramekins or glasses instead of one large bowl. Distribute the ingredients evenly among the ramekins.

STEP 4

STEP 4

STEP 5

STEP 7

STEP 8

RUM & RAISIN CRUNCH

I based this recipe on good old-fashioned brandysnaps and cream, which I can remember eating at fairgrounds as a child. You can use ready-made brandysnaps or make your own with the recipe given here.

SERVES 4

BRANDYSNAPS:
125 g/4 oz/¹/₂ cup butter
125 g/4 oz/¹/₂ cup caster (superfine) sugar
125 g/4 oz/¹/₃ cup golden (light corn) syrup
90 g/3 oz/³/₄ cup plain (all-purpose) flour, sifted
¹/₂ tsp ground ginger

RUM & RAISIN CREAM:
125 g/4 oz/²/₃ cup raisins
5 tbsp dark rum
5 tbsp water
150 ml/¹/₄ pint/²/₃ cup whipping cream
60 g/2 oz/¹/₄ cup Ricotta or full-fat soft cheese
30 g/1 oz/¹/₄ cup sifted icing (confectioners') sugar
30 g/1 oz/¹/₄ cup ground almonds
¹/₄ tsp almond flavouring (extract)
2 egg whites
6 brandysnaps, lightly crushed

1 To make the brandysnaps, put the butter, sugar and syrup into a saucepan and heat gently until melted.

2 Remove from the heat and mix in the flour and ginger until blended. Drop teaspoonfuls of the mixture on to a baking (cookie) sheet, leaving space to spread. Bake in a preheated oven at 180°C/350°F/Gas Mark 4 for about 8 minutes until golden brown.

3 Chill 4 ramekins or a serving bowl.

4 Put the raisins, rum and water into a saucepan and bring to the boil. Simmer for 5 minutes, then leave to rest for 20 minutes.

5 Whip the cream.

6 Press the soft cheese through a sieve (strainer) and stir in the icing (confectioners') sugar.

7 Fold in the whipped cream, ground almonds and flavouring (extract). Whisk the egg whites and fold them into the mixture.

8 Drain the raisins and stir them into the mixture with the crushed brandysnaps.

9 Spoon into the chilled dishes. Chill for at least 30 minutes.

STEP 1: Belle Hélène

STEP 2: Belle Hélène

STEP 1: Framboises

STEP 2: Framboises

COUPE AU CHOCOLAT

On a hot summer's day, there is nothing nicer than sitting in a pavement café and choosing from a whole menu of ice cream coupes, which are usually beautifully presented. Here are some quick ideas to liven up chocolate ice cream.

EACH RECIPE SERVES 4

COUPE BELLE HELENE:
250 g/8 oz/1 cup granulated sugar
250 ml/8 fl oz/1 cup water
3 pears, peeled, quartered and cored
125 g/4 oz/4 squares dark chocolate
chocolate ice cream
whipped double (heavy) cream (optional)

1 Put the sugar and water into a saucepan and bring to the boil. Simmer for 5 minutes and add the pears. Simmer gently for 10 minutes, or until the pears are tender. Very ripe pears will not take as long. Set the pears aside and drain off half of the syrup.

2 Break up the chocolate and add it to the syrup in the saucepan. Stir until smooth, about 3–4 minutes.

3 To serve, put 3 scoops of ice cream into each serving dish or coupe, and spoon over 3 pear quarters. Pour a little chocolate syrup over the whole and pipe some cream on top, if liked.

COUPE AUX FRAMBOISES:
250 g/8 oz can raspberries in syrup or
* 250 g/8 oz/1¹/₃ cups raspberries, fresh or frozen*

about 3 tbsp icing (confectioners') sugar
chocolate ice cream
whipped double (heavy) cream (optional)
ice cream wafers

1 If you are using canned raspberries, purée them in a blender or food processor, or mash them well with a wooden spoon.

2 If using fresh raspberries, purée them in a blender or food processor, or mash them well with a wooden spoon, and press through a sieve (strainer). Sift in icing (confectioners') sugar to taste.

3 To serve, put 3 scoops of ice cream in each chilled serving dish or coupe, and pour the raspberry sauce over the top. Pipe whipped cream on the top if liked and serve with wafers.

VARIATION

Other instant sauces can be whipped up by puréeing a can of blackcurrants in syrup or strawberries in syrup, and serving with ice cream of your choice.

CHAPTER TWO

Hot Puddings

A cold winter's night is the best time to enjoy a hot pudding without feeling guilty – after all, we have to keep the cold out somehow! There is no better way to do this than with a comforting Italian Bread & Butter Pudding, and Granny Bob's Chocolate Pudding is guaranteed to warm a few hearts. Even if you don't need to count the calories, you may be pleased to know that the New Age Spotted Dick has very little cholesterol, thanks to a reworking of the original recipe.

Not all hot puddings need be substantial and filling; if you prefer a lighter hot pudding, try the Magic Lemon Pudding or Almond Pancakes with Fruit Coulis.

Opposite: *Hot puddings are the ultimate comfort food, and chocolate is often a key ingredient. Use a high-quality chocolate for the best results.*

STEP 1

STEP 2

STEP 3

STEP 4

MAGIC LEMON PUDDING

This light dessert magically separates in the oven to form a thick lemon sauce base and a spongy topping. My mother was baking this in the Fifties, and now it has become fashionable again!

SERVES 4–6

90 g/ 3 oz/¹⁄₃ cup granulated sugar
30 g/ 1 oz/¹⁄₄ cup plain (all-purpose) flour
2 egg yolks
15 g/¹⁄₂ oz/ 1 tbsp butter
finely grated rind of 1 lemon
4 tbsp lemon juice
250 ml/ 8 fl oz/ 1 cup milk
2 egg whites

TO DECORATE:
icing (confectioners') sugar
grated lemon rind

1 Sift the sugar and flour together into a bowl.

2 Stir in the egg yolks, butter and lemon rind and juice. Beat together thoroughly.

3 Stir in the milk and whisk well.

4 Whisk the egg whites until stiff and fold in well.

5 Spoon the mixture into an attractive 1 litre/1³⁄₄ pint/4 cup ovenproof serving dish.

6 Put the dish into a roasting tin (pan) half-filled with water and bake in a preheated oven at 180°C/ 350°F/Gas Mark 4 for 35 minutes.

7 Sprinkle with grated lemon rind and dust with icing (confectioners') sugar. Serve immediately from the dish.

WHISKING EGG WHITES

When whisking egg whites, start slowly, using a figure-of-eight motion, until the whites are a mass of bubbles, then speed up gradually. If using a balloon whisk, you may find it comfortable to sit the bowl on your left hip and whisk with the right arm, or vice versa. Electric whisks are a lot quicker but they do not achieve such a large volume from the egg whites as a traditional hand whisk would. Using a copper bowl reacts with the egg whites to make them stronger, more long-lasting and resilient, which is useful when the egg whites are being folded into a mixture. Make sure the bowl is completely dry and free of grease, as even a little water or grease will make the whites harder to beat to a good 'froth'.

STEP 2

STEP 3

STEP 4

STEP 5

GRANNY BOB'S CHOCOLATE PUDDING

A deliciously moist pudding, served piping hot to the table. Softly whipped cream is a wonderful addition.

SERVES 4–6

60 g/2 oz/¹/₄ cup butter, softened
125 g/4 oz/¹/₂ cup caster (superfine) sugar
60 g/2 oz/2 squares dark chocolate, broken
  into pieces
2 eggs, lightly beaten
125 g/4 oz/1 cup self-raising flour

SAUCE:
300 ml/¹/₂ pint/1¹/₄ cups milk
60 g/2 oz/¹/₄ cup butter
60 g/2 oz/2 squares dark chocolate, broken
  into pieces
3 tbsp granulated sugar
2 tbsp golden (light corn) syrup

1 Grease a 1.1 litre/2 pint/4¹/₂ cup pudding basin. In a separate bowl, beat the butter and sugar together until pale.

2 Meanwhile, melt the chocolate in a bowl set over a pan of barely simmering water. This should take about 10 minutes. Stir into the butter mixture.

3 Beat in the eggs, one at a time, beating well after each addition.

4 Sift the flour into the bowl and fold in thoroughly.

5 Put all the sauce ingredients into a saucepan and heat through gently, without boiling, for about 10 minutes, until the chocolate has melted. Whisk well to combine.

6 Pour the sponge mixture into the greased pudding basin and pour the sauce over the top.

7 Bake in a preheated oven at 190°C/ 375°F/Gas Mark 5 for about 40 minutes, and serve piping hot from the bowl, or turned out on to a serving dish.

MELTING CHOCOLATE

Chocolate must be melted slowly in order to prevent it from 'seizing', which results in the chocolate being very granular and unworkable. To avoid this, chocolate must not come into contact with droplets of water or be heated to too high a temperature too quickly – treat chocolate with care.

ITALIAN BREAD & BUTTER PUDDING

This was created at one of those times when I was forced to improvise through lack of ingredients! Isn't it strange how those desserts are often the best?

STEP 2

STEP 4

STEP 5

STEP 6

SERVES 4–6

90 g/3 oz/¹⁄₃ cup unsalted butter, softened
200 g/7 oz/7 slices white bread
90 g/3 oz/¹⁄₂ cup raisins
2 tbsp almond liqueur, such as Amaretto
125 g/4 oz/1 cup coarsely crushed ratafias,
*   macaroons, or amaretti biscuits (cookies)*
30 g/1 oz/3 tbsp cut mixed (candied) peel
600 ml/1 pint/2¹⁄₂ cups milk
¹⁄₄ tsp vanilla flavouring (extract)
90 g/3 oz/¹⁄₃ cup caster (superfine) sugar
2 eggs, lightly beaten
45 g/1¹⁄₂ oz/¹⁄₃ cup soft light brown sugar

1 Grease a 25 × 20 cm/10 × 8 inch baking dish with some of the butter.

2 Spread the remaining butter on to the bread.

3 Combine the raisins, liqueur and 2 tablespoons of water in a small saucepan and bring to a gentle boil, then set aside for 30 minutes.

4 Leave the crusts on the bread slices and cut each slice diagonally into 4. Use half of the bread to make a layer in the bottom of the dish, overlapping in rows.

5 Sprinkle with half of the ratafias, half the soaked raisins and half the mixed (candied) peel. Repeat with the remaining half of the ingredients.

6 Heat the milk through gently with the vanilla flavouring (extract), until the surface quivers and it is nearly boiling. Remove from the heat and stir in the caster (superfine) sugar and eggs. Spoon the milk mixture over the whole bread dish. Sprinkle over the brown sugar.

7 Bake in a preheated oven at 180°C/350°F/Gas Mark 4 for 30 minutes. Serve immediately, piping hot from the dish.

VARIATIONS

For a variation, try adding dried fruit, such as apricots, cherries or dates, to the Bread & Butter Pudding. Another delicious alternative is to use malted milk, made up from a malted hot drink powder, in place of the ordinary milk.

NEW AGE SPOTTED DICK

This a deliciously moist low-fat pudding. The sauce is in the centre of the pudding, and will spill out when the pudding is cut. Serve with custard for a richer pudding.

STEP 3

SERVES 6–8

140 g/4¹/₂ oz/³/₄ cup raisins
140 ml/4¹/₂ fl oz/generous ¹/₂ cup corn oil,
  plus a little for brushing
140 g/4¹/₂ oz/generous ¹/₂ cup caster
  (superfine) sugar
30 g/1 oz/¹/₄ cup ground almonds
2 eggs, lightly beaten
175 g/6 oz/1¹/₂ cups self-raising flour

SAUCE:
60 g/2 oz/¹/₂ cup chopped walnuts
60 g/2 oz/¹/₂ cup ground almonds
300 ml/¹/₂ pint/1¹/₄ cups milk (semi-
  skimmed may be used)
4 tbsp granulated sugar

1 Put the raisins in a saucepan with 120 ml/4 fl oz/¹/₂ cup water. Bring to the boil, then remove from the heat. Leave to steep for 10 minutes, then drain.

2 Whisk together the oil, sugar and ground almonds until thick and syrupy; this will need about 8 minutes of beating (on medium speed if using an electric whisk).

3 Add the eggs, one at a time, beating well after each addition.

4 Combine the flour and raisins. Stir into the mixture.

5 Brush a 1 litre/1³/₄ pint/4 cup pudding basin with oil, or line with baking parchment.

6 Put all the sauce ingredients into a saucepan. Bring to the boil, stir and simmer for 10 minutes.

7 Transfer the sponge mixture to the greased basin and pour on the hot sauce. Place on a baking (cookie) sheet.

8 Bake in a preheated oven at 170°C/340°F/Gas Mark 3¹/₂ for about 1 hour. Lay a piece of baking parchment across the top if it starts to brown too fast.

9 Leave to cool for 2–3 minutes in the basin before turning out on to a serving plate.

STEP 4

STEP 5

> ### RAISINS
>
> I always soak raisins before baking them, as they retain their moisture nicely and you taste the flavour of them instead of biting on a dried-out raisin.

STEP 6

STEP 2

STEP 4

STEP 5

STEP 6

ALMOND PANCAKES WITH FRUIT COULIS

I designed this dessert for the times when something hot but not necessarily heavy or too filling is called for – Boxing Day perhaps!

SERVES 4–8

30 g/1 oz/¼ cup flaked (slivered) almonds
125 g/4 oz/1 cup plain (all-purpose) flour
1 egg
1 egg yolk
300 ml/½ pint/1¼ cups milk
30 g/1 oz/2 tbsp butter, melted
4 tbsp ground almonds, lightly toasted
¼ tsp almond flavouring (extract)
oil for brushing
250 g/8 oz/1½ cups frozen mixed summer
     fruits, such as redcurrants, blackcurrants
     and raspberries
2 tbsp icing (confectioners') sugar
400 g/14 oz can of guavas in syrup, or
     other fruit of your choice

1 Spread out the flaked (slivered) almonds on a baking sheet and toast them in a preheated oven at 180°C/350°F/Gas Mark 4 for 3 minutes.

2 Sift the flour into a bowl and make a well in the centre. Add the egg, egg yolk, milk, melted butter, ground almonds and almond flavouring (extract). Whisk well to combine. Leave to rest for 30 minutes.

3 Brush a frying pan (skillet) or pancake pan with oil and place over a medium heat. Tilt the pan (skillet) in one direction and pour in 50 ml/ 2 fl oz/¼ cup of the batter. Tilt in the opposite direction immediately, so that the batter covers the whole base. After 1–2 minutes, or when the top of the pancake starts to dry out, toss it and cook on the other side for about 1 minute. Repeat with the remaining batter.

4 Transfer the pancakes to a baking (cookie) sheet lined with baking parchment, cover and keep warm in a preheated oven at 150°C/300°F/Gas Mark 3.

5 Blend the fruit in a blender or food processor, or mash it well by hand, with 2 tablespoons of water. Press through a sieve (strainer) and stir in the icing (confectioners') sugar. Warm the fruit coulis through over a medium heat.

6 Warm the guavas through, in their own syrup, over a medium heat.

7 Fold each pancake twice and place 1 or 2 on each serving plate. Lift the top layer of each pancake and spoon in the warmed guavas and decorate with the toasted almonds. Pour a little fruit coulis over the top.

TARTE TATIN

The classic Tarte Tatin, or upside-down cake, is made with apples; here I have used pears which, I'm sure you will agree, are equally delicious!

STEP 2

STEP 3

STEP 4

STEP 6

SERVES 4–6

PASTRY:
125 g/4 oz/¹/₂ cup unsalted butter, softened
90 g/3 oz/¹/₃ cup caster (superfine) sugar
1 egg, lightly beaten
250 g/8 oz/2 cups plain (all-purpose) flour
salt

PEAR TOPPING:
30 g/1 oz/2 tbsp butter
60 g/2 oz/¹/₃ cup light brown sugar
1 tbsp lemon juice
1 kg/2 lb dessert (eating) pears

1 First make the pastry. Beat the butter and caster (superfine) sugar together until light and fluffy.

2 Add the egg and beat well. Add the flour gradually with a pinch of salt and mix to a smooth dough. Knead lightly for 5 minutes. Wrap and chill for at least 2 hours.

3 Line the base of a 23 cm/9 inch cake tin (pan) with baking parchment. Spread half the butter and brown sugar over the bottom.

4 Add the lemon juice to a large bowl of water. Peel, core and quarter the pears, putting them into the acidulated water as you go. When all the pears are prepared, drain off the water thoroughly, and pat the fruit dry with paper towels. Pack them tightly into the bottom of the cake tin (pan).

5 Sprinkle with the remaining brown sugar and butter. Bake in a preheated oven at 220°C/425°F/Gas Mark 7 for 20 minutes, or until a light caramel forms.

6 When the pears are cooked, roll out the chilled dough into a 25 cm/10 inch circle on a floured work surface (counter). Work quickly at this stage, so that the butter in the dough does not melt. Use plenty of flour on both the work surface (counter) and the rolling pin. Do not worry about making the circle very neat as the tart is inverted, so any wrinkles will not show. Place the dough over the pears.

7 Bake in a preheated oven at 200°C/400°F/Gas Mark 6 for about 20 minutes, or until well browned.

8 Remove from the oven and invert on a warmed serving plate. Serve at once with clotted cream or ice cream.

CHAPTER THREE

Cold Puddings

Sometimes a substantial cold dessert is required for a party or buffet or to round off a light meal. Here are a few ideas, all of which can be made in advance and stored in the refrigerator for up to 3 days. The Summer Pudding will last longer, up to 6 days.

Personally, I love a good Sherry Trifle and there are few who don't, but everybody has their own recipe and this is mine. Trifles often have jelly set in the base, which is a variation on the original recipe; I'm not very keen on this, so my recipe follows the traditional path, which I think you will prefer.

Summer Pudding, of course, is a perennial favourite. It is best made in late summer when fresh blackberries are available – and, in some areas, wild strawberries – which add lots of flavour. Serve simply with clotted or single (light) cream.

Tiramisù has many imitators, but the only way to get the unique flavour and texture is to use Mascarpone cheese, stirred into the cream; otherwise it becomes simply a chocolate trifle.

Opposite: *The simplest ingredients can make the most elegant puddings. Choose ingredients that are at their peak for the best flavour and appearance.*

STEP 1

STEP 2

STEP 3

STEP 5

SUMMER PUDDING

Use whatever summer fruit you have available. Strawberries do not give such a good result, but cherries are delicious when included in the mixture. Good quality frozen fruit can now be bought all year round.

SERVES 4–6

1 kg/2 lb mixed summer fruit, such as blackberries, redcurrants, blackcurrants, raspberries, loganberries and cherries
175 g/6 oz/³/₄ cup caster (superfine) sugar
8 small slices white bread
clotted cream or single (light) cream, to serve

1 Stir the fruit and sugar together in a large saucepan, cover and bring to the boil. Simmer for 10 minutes, stirring once.

2 Cut the crusts off the bread slices.

3 Line a 1.1 litre/2 pint/4¹/₂ cup pudding basin with the bread.

4 Add the fruit and as much of the cooking juices as will fit into the bread-lined bowl.

5 Cover the fruit with the remaining bread slices.

6 Put the pudding basin on to a large plate or a shallow baking (cookie) sheet. Place a plate on top and weigh it down with cans.

7 Chill overnight, or for up to 6 days.

8 When ready to serve, turn the pudding out on to a serving plate or shallow bowl and serve cold with clotted cream or single (light) cream.

VARIATION

To give the pudding a more lasting set, dissolve 2 sachets (envelopes) or 2 tablespoons of powdered gelatine in water and stir into the fruit mixture. This enables you to turn it out on to the serving plate a couple of hours before serving.

STEP 2

STEP 4

STEP 5

STEP 6

WHITE & DARK CHOCOLATE MOUSSE

Although this looks stunning, it is in fact very simple to make, with the aid of a couple of large bowls and a good hand whisk.

SERVES 6–8

100 g/3¹/₂ oz/3¹/₂ squares dark chocolate
100 g/3¹/₂ oz/3¹/₂ squares good quality
*   white chocolate*
4 egg yolks
2 tbsp brandy
1 sachet (envelope) or 1 tbsp powdered
*   gelatine*
50 ml/2 fl oz/¹/₄ cup hot water
300 ml/¹/₂ pint/1¹/₄ cups double (heavy)
*   cream*
4 egg whites

TO DECORATE:
100 g/3¹/₂ oz/3¹/₂ squares good quality
*   white or dark chocolate*
1 tbsp lard (shortening)
cocoa powder

1 Break the dark and white chocolate into pieces and put them into separate heatproof bowls. Set the bowls over saucepans of barely simmering water and melt the chocolate.

2 When melted, remove the bowls and beat 2 egg yolks into each, until smooth. Stir the brandy into the dark chocolate mixture. Set aside to cool, stirring the chocolate frequently.

3 Heat the gelatine and hot water in a heatproof bowl, set over a pan of barely simmering water, until it is clear, about 10 minutes. Stir half of the gelatine into each chocolate mixture until smooth.

4 Whip the cream until softly stiff, and whisk the egg whites until stiff.

5 Stir half of the cream into each chocolate mixture, then fold half of the egg whites into each mixture.

6 Pour or spoon both mousses at the same time into a 900 ml/1¹/₂ pint/ 3¹/₂ cup soufflé dish, one in each half of the dish, so that they meet in the middle but do not run into each other. Chill until ready to serve.

7 Break the chocolate for decorating into pieces and put into a heatproof bowl. Set over a pan of barely simmering water until melted, then stir in the lard (shortening) and pour into a small loaf tin (pan). Chill until set, then turn out.

8 To decorate, shave large curls of chocolate from the block with a vegetable peeler. Arrange attractively on the mousse, and dust with cocoa powder.

STEP 2

STEP 3

STEP 4

STEP 5

SHERRY TRIFLE

This is very similar to the recipe that Mrs Beeton made, which everyone knows and loves and which never fails to please. Use whatever fruit you have available, and, if you like, replace the Madeira (pound) cake with sponge fingers (lady-fingers) or sponge cake.

SERVES 4–6

60 g/2 oz/¹/₂ cup cornflour (cornstarch)
1.1 litres/2 pints/4¹/₂ cups milk
10 egg yolks
¹/₂ tsp almond flavouring (extract)
125 g/4 oz/¹/₂ cup caster (superfine) sugar
200 g/7 oz/6 inches Madeira (pound) cake, sliced
2 tbsp raspberry jam
250 ml/8 fl oz/1 cup sherry, sweet or dry, depending on taste
1¹/₂ tbsp chopped mixed nuts
2 × 425 g/14 oz cans of pineapple rings
10 glacé (candied) cherries

TO DECORATE:
300 ml/¹/₂ pint/1¹/₄ cups whipping cream
chopped angelica
flaked (slivered) almonds, toasted

1 First make the custard. Blend the cornflour (cornstarch) in a saucepan with a little of the milk to make a paste. Add the remaining milk and place over a medium heat. When it reaches boiling point, remove from the heat.

2 Meanwhile, beat together the egg yolks, almond flavouring (extract) and caster (superfine) sugar until pale.

Pour on the hot milk while beating continuously. Transfer to a clean pan and stir over a low heat for 5 minutes, or until thickened.

3 Put the slices of cake in the base of a glass trifle bowl. Spread thinly with the raspberry jam.

4 Sprinkle the sherry and then the nuts over the cake.

5 Arrange the pineapple rings around the edge of the bowl, flat against the glass. Put one glacé (candied) cherry in the centre of each pineapple ring.

6 Pour in the cooled custard without disturbing the pineapple rings, and chill until the custard is set.

7 To decorate, whip the cream until it is of piping consistency and pipe rosettes around the top of the trifle. Cut the angelica into squares and top each rosette with a square. Sprinkle the toasted flaked (slivered) almonds over the top, and serve.

CREME AUX MARRONS

The classic chestnut dessert is Mont Blanc, which is simply chestnuts and cream. This uses the same flavours with a bit of added zip!

STEP 1

SERVES 6

60 g/ 2 oz/ ⅓ cup sultanas (golden raisins)
3 tbsp orange-flavoured liqueur
finely grated rind of 1 orange
50 g/ 1¾ oz/ scant ¼ cup granulated sugar
75 ml/ 3 fl oz/ ⅓ cup orange juice
150 g/ 5 oz/ 1½ cups peeled chestnuts
   (canned or vacuum-packed)
300 ml/ ½ pint/ 1¼ cups double (heavy)
   cream
30 g/ 1 oz/ ¼ cup icing (confectioners')
   sugar

TO DECORATE:
candied oranges

1 Put the sultanas (golden raisins) into a small saucepan with the liqueur and the orange rind. Cover and bring to a gentle boil. Remove from the heat immediately and leave to steep for 10 minutes.

2 Put the granulated sugar and orange juice into a clean saucepan and bring to the boil, stirring until the sugar has dissolved. Add the chestnuts and poach over a low to medium heat for 10 minutes. Drain the chestnuts and reserve the cooking liquid.

3 Put the chestnuts into a blender with 3 tbsp of the cooking liquid. Blend until smooth; add more liquid if necessary. Alternatively, chop and mash the chestnuts and press them through a sieve (strainer) with 3 tablespoons of the cooking liquid. Add more liquid if necessary.

4 Whip the cream and sift in the icing (confectioners') sugar.

5 Put the cream into 1 piping bag and the chestnut mixture into another. Pipe alternate layers of whipped cream and chestnut mixture into 6 glasses, reserving a little of the cream for decoration. Alternatively, spoon into the glasses. The dessert is very rich, so small servings are fine. If you prefer, spoon the chestnut mixture into the glasses first, and top with the cream.

6 Spoon the raisins over the top. Decorate with chopped, candied orange and a rosette of the whipped cream.

STEP 2

STEP 3

STEP 4

BANOFFI PIE

This is something that my grandmother used to make and it is just as delicious today. It is becoming increasingly popular, and turns up on restaurant menus and in cafés quite regularly. Thanks to the condensed milk, it is deliciously sticky.

STEP 2

STEP 4

STEP 6

STEP 8

SERVES 6–8

400 g/ 14 oz can condensed milk
250 g/ 8 oz/ 2 cups plain (all-purpose) flour
125 g/ 4 oz/ ¹/₂ cup unsalted butter
8 tsp cold water
3 bananas
300 ml/ ¹/₂ pint/ 1¹/₄ cups double (heavy) cream
1 tsp instant coffee powder
1 tsp hot water

1 Leave the can of milk unopened and place it in a saucepan of water, so that it is submerged. Bring the water to the boil and boil the can for 4 hours.

2 Sift the flour into a bowl and rub in the butter until the mixture resembles breadcrumbs. Mix in the water and bring the mixture together lightly with your fingertips. Wrap in clingfilm (plastic wrap) or baking parchment and chill for at least 30 minutes.

3 Line a 25 cm/10 inch flan tin (pan) with baking parchment.

4 Roll out the pastry into a 25 cm/10 inch circle and line the flan tin (pan) with it.

5 Bake the pastry base in a preheated oven at 190°C/375°F/ Gas Mark 5 for 15 minutes. Leave to cool in the tin (pan).

6 Open the boiled can of condensed milk – if it is still hot, open it under a tea towel (dishcloth). The milk will have turned to a toffee-like consistency. Spread a single layer of the 'toffee' over the cooked pastry base.

7 Slice the bananas and spread out over the toffee layer.

8 Whip the cream until softly stiff. Dissolve the instant coffee powder in the hot water and fold into the cream.

9 Spoon or pipe the cream over the bananas. Chill until ready to serve.

BAKING DISH

If you are using a ceramic or non-metal pie dish, the pastry may not cook properly. To avoid this, preheat a baking (cookie) sheet in the oven for 10 minutes and place the pastry case (pie shell) on this before putting it in the oven.

STEP 1

STEP 2

STEP 3

STEP 4

TIRAMISU

Literally translated, this means 'pick-me-up' – a kick start of coffee, chocolate and alcohol!

SERVES 6–8

24 sponge fingers (lady-fingers) or
  savoiardi
5 tbsp instant coffee powder
300 ml/¹/₂ pint/1¹/₄ cups hot water
3 tbsp rum
300 ml/¹/₂ pint/1¹/₄ cups double (heavy)
  cream
250 g/8 oz/1 cup Mascarpone cheese
60 g/2 oz/¹/₃ cup icing (confectioners')
  sugar
2 tbsp cocoa powder

1 Cover the bottom of a pretty serving dish with half the sponge fingers (lady-fingers) or savoiardi.

2 Combine the instant coffee powder and hot water and soak the sponge fingers (lady-fingers) in half of the coffee and half of the rum for a few minutes.

3 Whip the cream, stir in the Mascarpone cheese and sift in the icing (confectioners') sugar.

4 Spoon half the Mascarpone cheese mixture in a layer over the sponge fingers (lady-fingers).

5 Sift half of the cocoa powder over the Mascarpone cheese mixture. Make another layer of sponge fingers (lady-fingers) in the same way, using the remaining coffee and rum, Mascarpone cheese mixture and cocoa powder.

6 Chill for at least 4 hours before serving.

HANDY HINT

Liquid instant coffee is ideal to use in place of instant coffee powder when baking. It can also be added to cakes to provide an instant coffee flavour.

CHAPTER FOUR

Light Desserts

Why is it that so many things that taste delicious are no good for your health? This needn't be so, and to prove it, I have put together some delicious and indulgent recipes that are kind to your health too. Rather than remove the good parts altogether, I have used supplements and substitutes wherever possible.

Low-fat alternatives and cream substitutes are easily available from supermarkets; these include crème fraîche, fromage frais, Quark, creamy yogurts and other dairy alternatives, along with all the low-fat versions of these products. Do examine the packaging, though, as some of these products can have a similar fat and calorie content to the real thing and need to be used in moderation.

Opposite: *Fresh fruit is often a key ingredient in light desserts. A combination of familiar and exotic fruits makes a dish as interesting to look at as it is to eat. Experiment with a range of ingredients to find your favourite combination.*

STEP 1

STEP 2

STEP 5

STEP 6

COEURS A LA CREME

This light dairy dessert is very well complemented by summer fruits and berries. It takes its name from the heart-shaped moulds in which it is traditionally served, but can be made in anything with a few holes in it, such as a sieve (strainer) lined with muslin (cheesecloth).

SERVES 4–6

250 g/8 oz/1 cup 20 per cent fat soft cheese (extra light) or Quark
300 ml/½ pint/1¼ cups double (heavy) cream
few drops vanilla flavouring (extract)
30 g/1 oz/¼ cup icing (confectioners') sugar
2 egg whites
400 g/13 oz can apricots in syrup

1 Line 4 moulds (or whatever you are using) with damp muslin (cheesecloth).

2 Press the soft cheese through a sieve (strainer).

3 Whip the cream until softly stiff and add the vanilla flavouring (extract) and sugar.

4 Blend well and stir into the soft cheese.

5 Whisk the egg whites until stiff. Spoon a quarter of them into the cream and blend well. Fold in the remaining whites.

6 Divide the mixture between the moulds and put them on a tray or plate. Leave to drain overnight in the refrigerator. At this stage they can be stored for up to 2 days in the refrigerator.

7 Blend the apricots and their syrup in a blender or food processor. Alternatively, press them through a sieve (strainer). Turn the moulds out on to a serving plate and serve with a little apricot coulis.

VARIATION

Raspberry coulis is also delicious with this dessert. Blend or process a 400 g/14 oz can of raspberries in syrup and sieve (strain). If fresh raspberries are available, put 250 g/8 oz/1½ cups into a saucepan with 2 tablespoons icing (confectioners') sugar. Simmer to dissolve the sugar, and sieve (strain). When cooled, serve with the Coeurs à la Crème.

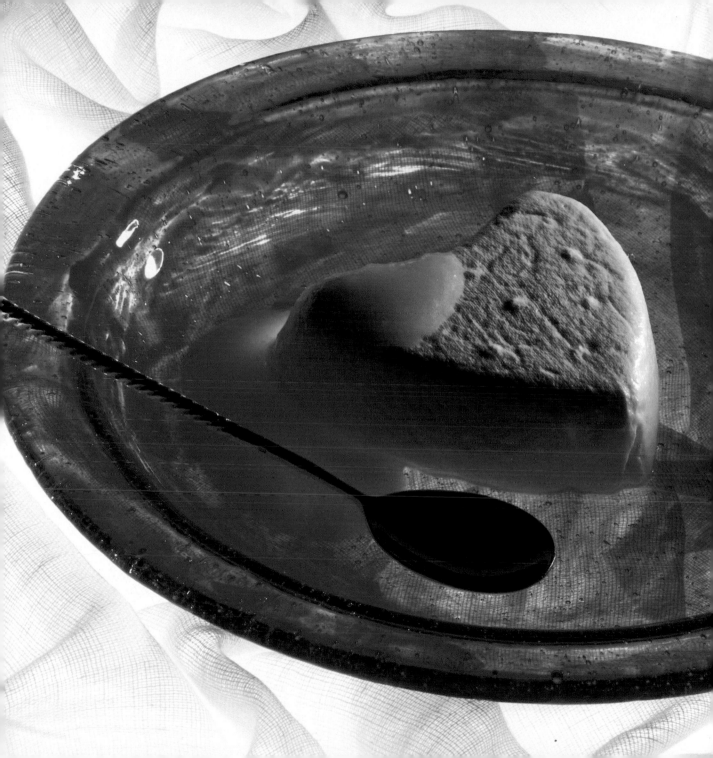

STEP 1

STEP 3

STEP 4

STEP 6

LIME FILO PARCELS

Everything can be prepared in advance for this light, tangy dessert. The syrup can be made and reheated, and the rolls can be either chilled or frozen and fried to finish. To ensure a light, crisp result, the oil should be hot, and the parcels drained on plenty of paper towels after frying.

SERVES 4–8

3 lemons, rinsed
3 limes, rinsed
1 tbsp finely chopped stem (candied) ginger
120 ml/4 fl oz/^{1}/$_2$ cup water
90 g/3 oz/^{1}/$_3$ cup granulated sugar
1 tsp cornflour (cornstarch)
3 sheets filo pastry
90 g/3 oz/^{3}/$_4$ cup pineapple, diced finely
90 g/3 oz/^{3}/$_4$ cup mango, diced finely
1 tbsp cornflour (cornstarch), mixed with
   enough cold water to make a paste
oil for deep frying (not olive oil)
desiccated (shredded) coconut, lightly
   toasted

1 First, make the syrup. Finely grate the rind and extract the juice from the lemons and limes, and put into a saucepan with the ginger, water and sugar. Bring to the boil and simmer for 5 minutes.

2 Put the 1 teaspoon of cornflour (cornstarch) into a small bowl and add a little water to make a paste. Stir in about 50 ml/2 fl oz/^{1}/$_4$ cup of the syrup, combine well and return to the saucepan. Bring to the boil, stirring. Remove from the heat and cover.

3 Spread out 1 sheet of the filo pastry on a work surface (counter), keeping the other 2 covered. Cut into 10 cm/4 inch squares.

4 Put a teaspoonful of the fruit in the middle of each square and roll up into a sausage shape, tucking the ends in. Seal the ends with the cornflour (cornstarch) paste.

5 Pour the oil to a depth of 6 cm/ 2^1/$_2$ inches into a deep frying pan (skillet) or wok and heat until it is 180°–190°C/350°–375°F or a cube of bread browns in 30 seconds. Have ready a plate or baking sheet lined with paper towels. Deep-fry the parcels until golden brown, 2–3 minutes, remove with a perforated spoon and drain on the paper towels. Keep warm while you fry the remaining parcels.

6 Put the desiccated (shredded) coconut on a plate and roll each parcel in it.

7 To serve, put 2 or 3 parcels on each plate, surrounded by the lemon and lime syrup.

STEP 2

STEP 3

STEP 4

STEP 6

STRAWBERRY MASCARPONE WITH SABLE BISCUITS (COOKIES)

A deliciously light dessert that would be a pleasure to eat at the end of a rich meal. The clean flavours would go very well with beef.

SERVES 4

BISCUITS (COOKIES):
150 g/ 5 oz/ 1¼ cups plain (all-purpose) flour
5 tbsp caster (superfine) sugar
90 g/ 3 oz/ ¹/₃ cup unsalted butter, softened
1 tbsp water
1 egg yolk

STRAWBERRY MASCARPONE:
2 egg yolks
60 g/ 2 oz/ ¹/₄ cup caster (superfine) sugar
500 g/ 1 lb/ 2 cups Mascarpone cheese
300 g/ 10 oz/ 2 cups strawberries, hulled
2 egg whites
icing (confectioners') sugar, to decorate

1 First, make the biscuits (cookies). Sift the flour into a bowl and stir in the sugar. Make a well in the centre and add the butter, water and egg yolk. Work with the fingertips until well blended, about 3 minutes. Roll into a ball and wrap in greaseproof paper (baking parchment). Chill for 1 hour.

2 Roll out the dough on a floured work surface (counter) until it is 5 mm/ ¹/₄ inch thick. Using a 6 cm/ 2¹/₂ inch cutter, stamp out about 20 biscuits (cookies).

3 Transfer the biscuits (cookies) to greased and floured or lined baking (cookie) sheets. Bake in a preheated oven at 180°C/350°F/Gas Mark 4 for 15–20 minutes. Transfer to a wire rack immediately.

4 Meanwhile, make the Strawberry Mascarpone. Beat together the egg yolks and sugar until pale.

5 Add the Mascarpone cheese and beat well.

6 Blend the strawberries in a blender or food processor. Sieve (strain) into a large bowl. Alternatively, mash the strawberries with a wooden spoon and press through a sieve (strainer). Stir in the Mascarpone cheese mixture.

7 Whisk the egg whites until stiff and fold into the Mascarpone cheese mixture.

8 To serve, place a spoonful or two of the strawberry Mascarpone on each serving plate, and place a few biscuits by the side. Dust with icing (confectioners') sugar.

EXOTIC FRUIT SALAD

This is a sophisticated fruit salad that makes use of some of the exotic fruits that can now be seen in the supermarket. It is delicious served with pancakes.

STEP 3

SERVES 6

3 passion-fruit
125 g/4 oz/¹/₂ cup caster (superfine) sugar
150 ml/¹/₄ pint/²/₃ cup water
1 mango
10 lychees, canned or fresh
1 star-fruit

1 Halve the passion-fruit and press the flesh through a sieve (strainer) into a saucepan.

2 Add the sugar and water to the saucepan and bring to a gentle boil, stirring frequently.

3 Put the mango on a chopping board and cut a thick slice from either side, cutting as near to the stone (pit) as possible. Cut away as much flesh as possible in large chunks from the stone (pit) section.

4 Take the 2 side slices and make 3 cuts through the flesh but not the skin, and 3 more at right angles to make a lattice pattern.

5 Push inside out so that the cubed flesh is exposed and you can easily cut it off.

6 Peel and stone (pit) the lychees and cut the star-fruit into 12 slices.

7 Add all the mango flesh, the lychees and the star-fruit to the passion-fruit and sugar syrup and poach gently for 5 minutes. Remove the fruit with a perforated spoon.

8 Bring the sugar syrup to the boil and cook for 5 minutes until it thickens slightly.

9 To serve, transfer all the fruit to a warmed serving bowl or individual serving glasses, pour over the sugar syrup, and serve warm, but not hot.

STEP 4

STEP 5

CARDAMOM CREAM

A delicious accompaniment to any exotic fruit dish is cardamom cream. Crush the seeds from 8 cardamom pods, add 300 ml/¹/₄ pint/1¹/₄ cups whipping cream and whip until soft peaks form.

STEP 7

STEP 2

STEP 3

STEP 4

STEP 5

MANGO MOUSSE

This delicious and exotic mousse can also be made with other tropical fruit such as paw-paw (papaya), pineapple or bananas.

SERVES 6–8

4 large ripe mangoes
1 passion-fruit
90 g/ 3 oz/ ⅓ cup caster (superfine) sugar
600 ml/ 1 pint/ 2½ cups thick natural
   yogurt or 300 ml/ ½ pint/ 1¼ cups thick
   natural yogurt and 300 ml/ ½ pint/ 1¼
   cups double (heavy) cream

1 To prepare the mango, set it on its side on a chopping board and cut a thick slice from each side as near to the stone (pit) as possible. Cut as much flesh away from the stone (pit) as possible, in large chunks. Take the 2 side slices and make 3 cuts through the skin but not the flesh, and make 3 more at right angles to make a lattice pattern. Push the skin inside out so that the cubed flesh is exposed and you can easily cut it off in large chunks.

2 Cut the passion-fruit in half and scoop out the flesh with a teaspoon. Sieve (strain) this and add it to the mango flesh.

3 Sprinkle the fruit with the sugar and leave to stand for 15–20 minutes.

4 Mash the fruit or blend it in a food processor or blender until smooth. Set aside a few spoonfuls for decoration.

5 Fold in the yogurt and blend well. Whip the cream, if using, and fold it into the mixture.

6 Chill the mousse for at least 2 hours until set. Spoon the reserved fruit purée over the mousse to serve.

MANGOES

Finding a really good mango in shops and supermarkets is quite an art. They are usually imported under-ripe and, as they don't have a chance to mature in the sun, may lose some of their sweetness and flavour. Even if they look and feel right the flesh may be disappointingly stringy or chalky. Look out for Bombay mangoes, which are the best I've ever eaten and are available all year round, although they are at their peak in March and April. Canned mangoes in syrup are a very good alternative if fresh ones are hard to find.

STEP 1

STEP 3

STEP 5

STEP 6

GRAPE & RICOTTA CHEESECAKE

A light and delicious cheesecake that is straightforward to make, and quick to disappear.

SERVES 6

90 g/ 3 oz/ $^3/_4$ cup digestive biscuits (graham crackers), crushed
125 g/ 4 oz/ 1 cup ratafia or amaretti biscuits (cookies), crushed
90 g/ 3 oz/ $^1/_3$ cup unsalted butter, melted and cooled
1 tbsp or 1 sachet (envelope) powdered gelatine
120 ml/ 4 fl oz/ $^1/_2$ cup double (heavy) cream
300 g/ 10 oz/ 1 $^1/_4$ cups Ricotta cheese
2 tbsp mixed (candied) peel
2 tbsp clear honey
$^1/_4$ tsp vanilla flavouring (extract)
350 g/ 12 oz/ 3 cups white (green) seedless grapes, washed

1 Combine the biscuits (crackers and cookies) and the butter. Press into the bottom of 6 ramekins or glasses, or into a 20 cm/ 8 inch springform tin (pan), and chill.

2 Put 3 tablespoons of hot water into a heatproof bowl, sprinkle on the powdered gelatine and stir. Set over a pan of barely simmering water and leave to dissolve. When it becomes clear, it is ready to use.

3 Whip the cream until stiff. Combine the Ricotta cheese, mixed (candied) peel, honey and vanilla flavouring (extract) in a separate bowl. Stir this mixture into the double (heavy) cream. Do not over-stir.

4 Stir the dissolved gelatine into the Ricotta mixture.

5 Halve the grapes. Divide half of them between the ramekins, glasses or tin (pan), arranging neatly on top of the biscuit (cracker and cookie) layer.

6 Spoon the Ricotta mixture over the top. Arrange the remaining grapes attractively on the top. Chill for 2 hours or until set.

7 To serve, remove the outer ring from the springform tin (pan), or put the ramekins on small plates.

VARIATION

The grapes in this recipe can be replaced by black grapes or any other fruit. Either canned or fresh apricots are particularly nice with this cheesecake.

CHAPTER FIVE

Special Occasion Desserts

What party would be complete without a grand finale, a dish that shows off your skills and sends your guests away satisfied and eager to return? Party desserts deserve a lot of effort and often need some advance preparation, but it will be worth it when you present your creation to your admiring guests.

When you are making your shopping list, think about how you will present the dish – which fruit to decorate it with, whether to use some confectionery or cake decorations, and perhaps a ribbon – anything to give it a bit of glamour! And think about the serving plate – I'm all for showing off the best china and bringing the best dishes out of the cupboard for such a special dessert – it is a compliment to your guests when you go to such trouble to entertain them.

CREME BRULEE

This is the classic recipe that everybody loves! The title simply means 'burned cream'.

STEP 1

STEP 3

STEP 4

STEP 7

SERVES 4

4 egg yolks
600 ml/ 1 pint/ 2¹/₂ cups double (heavy)
  cream
90 g/ 3 oz/¹/₃ cup light brown sugar

1 Beat the egg yolks until pale.

2 Put the cream into a saucepan and set over a medium heat. Bring it to boiling point for about 30 seconds.

3 Pour the cream on to the egg yolks, whisking all the time.

4 Return the cream and yolks to the saucepan, set over a gentle heat and stir until thickened, about 5 minutes.

5 Pour into individual ramekins or a large serving dish. Chill for 4 hours or overnight.

6 Sprinkle the brûlée with the light brown sugar to a thickness of about 5 mm/¹/₄ inch.

7 Place under a preheated very hot grill (broiler), until the sugar has caramelized to a golden brown. This takes about 3 minutes, depending on the heat of the grill (broiler), how far away from the grill (broiler) the brûlée is, and how thick the sugar is. Leave to cool before serving.

HANDY HINT

You may have seen a lozenge-shaped piece of iron on the end of a long handle in cook shops. This is a brûlée iron. It is usually about 7 cm/3 inches round and designed to be held flat over the brûlée, after being heated to a very high temperature over a flame or electric ring. The thickness of the iron means that it stays hot for a few minutes, long enough to caramelize the sugar.

STEP 1

STEP 2

STEP 3

STEP 4

HOT MOCHA SOUFFLE

Soufflés are not difficult, as long as your recipe is reliable and the mixture is right before you put it in the oven. The sauce here is a delightful addition to the recipe.

SERVES 6

butter for greasing
2 tbsp caster (superfine) sugar
2 egg yolks
3 tsp icing (confectioners') sugar
2 tsp plain (all-purpose) flour
150 g/5 oz/5 squares dark chocolate, melted
2 tsp instant coffee powder, dissolved in 1 tbsp hot water
4 egg whites
icing (confectioners') sugar, to decorate

SAUCE:
60 g/2 oz/¹/₄ cup granulated sugar
50 ml/2 fl oz/¹/₄ cup water
100 g/3¹/₂ oz/3¹/₂ squares dark chocolate
1 tbsp instant coffee powder
75 ml/3 fl oz/¹/₃ cup whipping cream

1 Butter a 900 ml/1¹/₂ pint/3¹/₂ cup soufflé dish. Dust with the caster (superfine) sugar and tap out any excess.

2 Beat the egg yolks until pale and sift in the icing (confectioners') sugar.

3 Stir in the flour, melted chocolate and dissolved coffee.

4 Wrap a piece of greaseproof paper or baking parchment around the soufflé dish, to an inch above the rim of the dish. Secure with string or an elastic band.

5 Whisk the egg whites until just stiff and fold into the soufflé mixture.

6 Pour the mixture into the soufflé dish right up to the rim. Run the tip of a knife quickly between the soufflé and the edge of the dish. Bake in a preheated oven at 180°C/350°F/Gas Mark 4 for 45 minutes. Do not open the oven.

7 Make the sauce. Put the sugar and water into a saucepan. Simmer until dissolved, then add the chocolate, instant coffee powder and cream. Keep warm until ready to serve.

8 To serve, transfer the sauce to a warmed serving jug and, working quickly, remove the parchment from the soufflé dish, dust with the icing (confectioners') sugar and take to the table before it sinks. Make a hole in the top of the soufflé by stabbing it with a knife, and pour in the sauce, preferably from a great height!

STEP 2

STEP 4

STEP 5

STEP 6

CHOCOLATE MARQUIS

A fabulously rich dessert that needs only a smidgen on each plate. If you feel it needs something else, serve with crème fraîche or fresh fruit, and make chocolate leaves to decorate.

SERVES 6–8

500 g / 1 lb dark chocolate
60 g / 2 oz / ¼ cup unsalted butter
30 g / 1 oz / 2 tbsp caster (superfine) sugar
4 whole eggs
1 tbsp plain (all-purpose) flour

1 Line a 20 cm / 8 inch springform tin (pan) with baking parchment.

2 Melt the chocolate, butter and half of the sugar together in a heatproof bowl set over a saucepan of barely simmering water.

3 Beat the eggs and remaining sugar together until pale. Fold in the flour carefully.

4 Pour the chocolate mixture on to the batter and stir in gently with a wooden spoon,

5 Fold together with a whisk, lightly, but until well combined.

6 Pour the mixture into the lined tin (pan) and bake in a preheated oven at 230°C/450°F/Gas Mark 8 for 12 minutes only. It should still be slightly wobbly in the centre.

7 Run a knife between the edge of the dessert and the tin (pan), and then release the tin (pan). Tighten the tin (pan) again, and leave the marquis in the tin (pan) to cool. Freeze for at least 2 hours or until required.

8 Remove from the freezer at least an hour before serving to allow the dessert to come to room temperature. Cut into small slices to serve.

CHOCOLATE LEAVES

Chocolate leaves make a very attractive decoration on the plate. Select some prettily shaped leaves from the garden and rinse them well. Drain and pat them dry with paper towels – they must be bone-dry. Melt some chocolate in the top of a double boiler or in a heatproof bowl set over a saucepan of simmering water. Use a grease-free paintbrush or pastry brush to brush the underside of the leaves with the melted chocolate. Make sure that the chocolate is thick where the leaf meets the stalk. Paint on 2 or 3 layers, just waiting for the chocolate to dry briefly between each layer. Spread them out on a tray to dry, and pop them into the freezer for 10 minutes to harden. When you are ready to use the chocolate leaves, simply peel the leaf from the chocolate.

STEP 3

STEP 4

STEP 5

STEP 6

BAKED ALASKA

This is another old favourite, and is a very impressive presentation that can be whipped up (literally!) at the last moment, and presented to admiring gasps. It is a pleasure to make too, because this recipe works so well.

SERVES 4–6

125 g/4 oz/¹/₂ cup butter, softened
125 g/4 oz/¹/₂ cup caster (superfine) sugar
2 eggs, lightly beaten
125 g/4 oz/1 cup self-raising flour
2 tbsp brandy or sherry
2 tbsp raspberry jam
900 ml/1¹/₂ pints/3¹/₂ cups vanilla or
    raspberry ripple ice cream – do not use
    'soft scoop' ice cream

MERINGUE:
4 egg whites
90 g/3 oz/¹/₃ cup caster (superfine) sugar

1 Grease and flour a 20 cm/8 inch sandwich cake tin (layer pan).

2 Beat the butter and sugar together, until pale and fluffy. Beat in the eggs gradually. If the mixture starts to separate while you are doing this, add a little flour and continue.

3 Fold in the flour carefully but thoroughly, and pour the mixture into the greased tin (pan). Bake in a preheated oven at 190°C/375°F/Gas Mark 5 for 40 minutes. Transfer to a wire rack to cool.

4 About 30 minutes before serving, transfer the sponge to an ovenproof serving dish, trimming to fit if necessary. Sprinkle with brandy and spread with the jam. Freeze for 20 minutes.

5 If the ice cream block is not round, transfer it to a plate and re-form it to the shape of your dish, using foil or greaseproof paper (baking parchment),

6 Remove the sponge from the freezer and put the ice cream on top. Re-freeze until 10 minutes before serving.

7 To make the meringue, whisk the egg whites until stiff. Add the caster (superfine) sugar gradually and continue whisking until stiff and glossy.

8 Take the sponge and ice cream from the freezer and cover the ice cream completely with the meringue mixture. Use the back of a spoon to form peaks all over. Work quickly so that the ice cream does not melt.

9 Bake in a preheated oven at 230°C/ 450°F/Gas Mark 8 for 5 minutes only. Keep an eye on it, as the meringue burns easily. Remove and serve immediately before the ice cream melts.

STEP 2

STEP 3

STEP 4

STEP 4

ZUCCOTTO

A delicious Italian trifle, very rich and very delicious! It can be prepared in advance and stored in the freezer, but remove at least 1 hour before serving so that it is relatively soft to eat.

SERVES 6–8

400 g/14 oz can of stoned (pitted) black
  cherries, drained, or 500 g/1 lb fresh
  black cherries, stoned (pitted)
2 tbsp maraschino
2 tbsp water
250 g/8 oz/6½ inches Madeira (pound)
  cake, thinly sliced, or 20 sponge fingers
3 tbsp orange-flavoured liqueur
600 ml/1 pint/2½ cups double (heavy)
  cream
90 g/3 oz/⅓ cup caster (superfine) sugar
¼ tsp vanilla flavouring (extract)
45 g/1½ oz/⅓ cup mixed (candied) peel
2 tbsp ground almonds
90 g/3 oz/3 squares dark chocolate, melted
2 tbsp rum
60 g/2 oz/½ cup hazelnuts, chopped

1 Put the cherries into a saucepan with the maraschino and water. Bring to the boil, remove from heat and leave to steep for 10 minutes.

2 Line the sides of a round 1.5 litre/ 2¾ pint/3 cup bowl with the sliced cake or sponge fingers. Drain the cherries and use the juice to moisten the sponge. Sprinkle the liqueur over the sponge. Put into the freezer.

3 Whip one third of the cream until stiff and stir in half of the sugar, the vanilla flavouring (extract), mixed (candied) peel and ground almonds. Spread this mixture in a layer over the sponge base and up the sides. Return to the freezer for 40 minutes until firm.

4 Whip one third of the cream until softly stiff, and fold in the cooled melted chocolate, the rum and hazelnuts. Spread this in a layer over the cream layer and return to the freezer.

5 Purée the cherries in a food processor, or mash well by hand, and stir in the rest of the sugar. Whip the remaining cream until stiff and fold in the cherries. Fill the centre of the bowl with this. Return to the freezer for 1 hour, or until ready to serve. If it is kept for longer than 2 hours in the freezer, remove 1 hour before serving. If you do not have a freezer, add a little powdered gelatine to the zuccotto. Dissolve 2 tablespoons or 2 sachets (envelopes) in 120 ml/4 fl oz/½ cup of hot water in a bowl set over a saucepan of simmering water. Stir a third of this into each layer.

6 To serve, unmould on to a chilled dish and decorate as you wish.

PAVLOVA

This fruit meringue dish was created for Anna Pavlova, and it looks very impressive. Be sure to use some of the fabulous fruits that are now available all year round, to make a colourful fruit display.

STEP 2

STEP 3

STEP 5

STEP 6

SERVES 8

6 egg whites
¹/₂ tsp cream of tartar
250 g/8 oz/1 cup caster (superfine) sugar
1 tsp vanilla flavouring (extract)
300 ml/¹/₂ pint/1¹/₄ cups whipping cream
400 g/13 oz/2¹/₂ cups strawberries, hulled and halved
3 tbsp orange-flavoured liqueur
fruit of your choice, to decorate

1 Line a baking (cookie) sheet with baking parchment and mark out a circle to fit your serving plate. The recipe makes enough meringue for a 30 cm/12 inch circle.

2 Whisk the egg whites and cream of tartar together until stiff. Gradually beat in the caster (superfine) sugar and vanilla flavouring (extract). Whisk well until glossy and stiff.

3 Either spoon or pipe the meringue mixture into the marked circle, in an even layer, slightly raised at the edges, to form a dip in the centre.

4 Baking the meringue depends on your preference. If you like a soft chewy meringue, bake at 140°C/275°F/Gas Mark 4 for about 1¹/₂ hours until dry but slightly soft in the centre. If you prefer a dry meringue, bake in the oven at 110°C/225°F/Gas Mark ¹/₄ for 3 hours until dry.

5 When you are ready to serve, whip the cream to a piping consistency, and either spoon or pipe on to the meringue base, leaving a border of meringue all around the edge.

6 Stir the strawberries and liqueur together and spoon on to the cream. Decorate with fruit of your choice, such as slices of mango, apple or pineapple. Serve immediately.

MAKING A DRY MERINGUE

I prefer a dry meringue and I leave it in the oven, on the lowest setting, overnight – however, I wouldn't recommend using this technique with a gas oven. In an electric oven or solid fuel cooker it would be fine.

PERFECT PUDDINGS

There are a number of basic ingredients that are regularly used in the making of puddings and desserts. Here is some detailed information about a few of them, which will help your puddings to turn out perfectly.

EGGS
Size 3 eggs are used throughout the recipes, unless stated – these weigh 60–65 g/ 2 oz in the shell.

Freshness
Eggs can be used up to 3–4 weeks after laying. However, it is difficult to tell from the date on the box how fresh an egg is, as they may have been laid well before packing.

A simple way to identify a really fresh egg is to hold it close to your ear – there will be no discernible movement. If it is a little older, you will hear some movement. However, this is not an exact indication of its age, only a rough guide, and the egg is fit to eat even if you can hear some movement.

A newly laid egg fills the entire shell, and as it ages, the air pocket at the broader end expands. This is the basis for the flotation test. A newly laid egg will lie on the bottom of a bowl of water; the older it is, the higher one end will sit in the water, until at two to three weeks old it is standing upright on the base of the bowl. If the whole egg floats, it should be discarded.

THE HISTORY OF PUDDINGS
At the conclusion of a meal when our appetites are usually satisfied and our palates content, a dessert offers a chance to indulge in something eaten purely for pleasure rather than nutrition, and offers the cook a chance to be creative and show off a little imagination and expertise.

The dessert course can take many forms. Sometimes a simple fruit bowl is enough; alternatively, fruit can be left to soak in sugar to bring out the full flavours and then adorned with cream. At the other extreme a skilful assembly of beautifully baked sponge, frozen cream and quickly cooked snowy egg white is designed to impress and will satisfy the eye and the mouth, as well as the cook's creative tendencies.

Desserts were not always so wide-ranging. Flummery – a fruit porridge – used to be the closest thing to a dessert that most people tasted, until sugar became more widely available, and entered into general use.

By the Victorian times refined sugar was available to most kitchens in well-to-do households, where the cook didn't hesitate to demonstrate his or her skills. This usually resulted in elaborate presentations of jellies and table creams, layered in different colours and moulded into fanciful shapes, designed to impress the eye more than satisfy the palate. After the grand designs of the Victorian era, we became more used to consuming sugar as part of our daily diet. Fudge and toffee were common and traditional puddings such as Sussex Pond Puddings, Bakewell Tart and Burnt Cream appeared quite regularly.

THE MODERN DESSERT
Depending on your preference, or the occasion, the dessert can be a light finish to a heavy meal, or a grand finale to finish a complex and creative meal. You may need to cater for children's simpler tastes at a family meal, whereas at an adult dinner table, something more sophisticated is called for. I know cooks who never present less than three desserts, and I have to say that I also enjoy the preparation and decoration that goes into the dessert course – it is an opportunity to show off your skill in the kitchen, and satisfy and delight your guests.

The season is a factor too, of course. There is nothing nicer in the middle of winter than to finish a simple meal with a hot dessert, where the dessert is actually providing some of the meal's nutritional content. The Italian Bread & Butter Pudding is ideal for this, as is the New Age Spotted Dick, or the Cherry Clafoutis in the 'Quick & Easy' section.

Although most berries are available all year round, fresh or frozen, they taste best when eaten at the height of summer with only a sprinkling of sugar.

A Baked Alaska will delight at any time of the year – children are especially thrilled to cut into the crisp meringue and find ice cream in the middle!

There is something here for the chocaholics among you – for a quick fix try the Chocolate Coconut Layer, or for something worth some extra effort, the Chocolate Marquis is fabulous!

When presenting rich desserts, I find that a large plate of fruit, peeled and cut, goes down extremely well as a refresher and palate cleanser, rather than the final savoury course of a titbit such as Welsh Rarebit or fritters that might have been served at a Victorian table.

INGREDIENTS
Even though we eat a huge variety of sweet and sugar products nowadays, the main ingredients for a dessert are usually varying amounts of a few basic ingredients, which are discussed below, with alternatives suggested where appropriate. Sometimes we need to satisfy a sweet tooth or create a dessert without stocking up on calories and cholesterol, and there are usually substitutes that can be used instead of the richer ingredients. I have detailed these below.

Butter
When baking or cooking with fat, butter has the finest flavour. If possible, it is best to use unsalted butter as an ingredient in puddings and desserts, unless stated otherwise in the recipe. Margarine can be substituted for butter if you prefer. However, do not use a 'low-fat spread' as a substitute, as most of them are not suitable for cooking with, especially if you are baking the dish; use plain margarine or a similar product, which states on the pack that it is suitable for baking. In some instances margarine will be more suitable, as it creams with sugar more pleasantly than butter.

Chocolate
There are chefs called *chocolatiers* who devote their working lives to perfecting the art of cooking with chocolate, creating desserts, sauces, confectionery, decorations, and even chocolate sculptures. However, you do not need a lifetime's experience to use chocolate to great effect.

Avoid using cake-covering products, as they will ruin the taste of your desserts. When testing these recipes, I used a good-quality dark or white eating chocolate, such as Lindt. Supermarkets' own brands are usually of a good quality too. The chocolate that professional chocolatiers use is called *couverture* chocolate and is bought in 5 kg/10 lb sizes. There are small bars of *couverture* available in most supermarkets, labelled *Chocolat Meunier*. The advantage of using this chocolate is that it has a higher cocoa solids content and is therefore more stable to work with and has a more satisfying chocolate taste.

Good-quality white chocolate has no cocoa solids content, only cocoa butter, which makes it a little more tricky to work with, but if you follow the recipe, you won't have a problem.

To melt chocolate, first break it into pieces. I do this by leaving the chocolate in the packet and banging it on the counter a few times. Obviously the smaller the pieces, the quicker it will melt. Use a heatproof glass or ceramic bowl to melt the chocolate in – a metal

Storage
Egg shells are porous, so eggs should not be stored near strong-smelling food.

Usage
Fresher eggs are more suitable for poaching and frying, as they stay more compact and the white is thicker in consistency. Older eggs are no less nutritious but are better kept for baking and sauces, where appearance is not necessarily a consideration, as the white of the egg becomes more fluid and watery.

Duck and goose eggs are eminently suitable for baking as they have a higher fat content than hen eggs. They have an average weight of 90 g/3 oz, which should be taken into account when using them in place of hen eggs.

Whisking
There is no trick or mystery to whisking egg whites to a maximum foam, but the best results are obtained if a few simple precautions are taken.

First, separate the egg whites from the yolks by dropping the whites into a small bowl, then transferring each white to the whisking bowl as you go. This ensures that any stray bits of egg yolk will spoil only one white.

The foam is formed by air being enveloped by the protein in the egg white. Acid helps the protein to stretch and make a larger volume of foam, which is why a pinch of cream of tartar is often added at the beginning of whisking.

A hand-held balloon whisk gets the best results from egg whites, whereas electric mixers do the job quickly and efficiently, but without creating as much volume as a balloon whisk would.

You should select a large bowl, so that there is enough space for you to whisk, and for the whites to expand, and make sure the bowl is free of grease. Many chefs use unlined copper bowls to whisk in, as a harmless chemical reaction between the copper and egg whites creates a stronger and more stable foam.

Start by whisking slowly in a figure-of-eight pattern until the whites are a mass of bubbles, then speed up your whisking, lifting and enveloping air as you go. When the whisk leaves a soft peak when it is lifted, the whites are the right consistency for folding into most mixtures, including soufflés and omelettes. If you are using the whites for meringues, carry on whisking until the whisk leaves a stiff peak. Do not stop whisking once you have started, and be careful not to overbeat the whites – they will become grainy and unusable.

If you are adding sugar, whisk it in gradually until the whites are stiff and glossy. Use the beaten whites immediately so that they lose no air.

bowl can be used, but it often gets too hot, and for this reason needs constant attention. The bowl must be set over a saucepan so that it fits tightly at the top; this prevents steam from escaping and dripping into the chocolate, which will make the chocolate 'seize' or become granular, at which point it must be abandoned, as it cannot be recovered.

Chocolate can also be melted in the microwave on High Power, and should be stirred every 30 seconds.

When adding other ingredients to chocolate, avoid adding alcohol first to neat chocolate; add the other ingredients first, and the alcohol last. If you have to add alcohol first, pour it all in at once and stir constantly until smooth.

Cocoa powder

This can be used as a flavouring in place of chocolate, but the liquid content of the dish must be increased to compensate. This is usually done by adding milk, as milk has a fat content that helps to create the right consistency.

Cream

This most delicious ingredient comes in various forms:

Clotted cream – This was once available only in the West Country of England, but is now widely available from supermarkets. It has a 55 per cent fat content and is very thick. It is suitable for serving with a wide variety of desserts, and in Cornwall is served with ice cream!

Crème fraîche – This is a cream product that is becoming increasingly popular.

Originally from France, it has a slightly sour, nutty taste and is very thick. It is suitable for cooking, but has the same fat content as double (heavy) cream. It can be made by stirring cultured buttermilk into double (heavy) cream and refrigerating overnight.

Double (heavy) cream – This is the only cream that can safely be boiled without curdling. Typically it is 48 per cent saturated fat, which is bad news for people who have to monitor cholesterol levels – there are substitutes suggested below. Double (heavy) cream can be whipped to a large volume, but 'extra thick' double (heavy) cream is not suitable for whipping.

Half cream – This is not suitable for cooking and should be used only in coffee and for pouring over desserts. It has a 12 per cent fat content.

Longlife cream – This is suitable for use in cooking, but the flavour is quite different. The taste is often artificial instead of authentically creamy.

Single (light) cream – This is the type of cream most commonly used for cooking; however, this kind of cream should not be boiled, as it will curdle. Also, always add hot liquids to the cream rather than the cream to the liquids, to avoid curdling. Single (light) cream can be stirred into cake mixes and poured on to desserts and into coffee. Unpasteurized cream has a lot more flavour than the modern pasteurized version, but is only available direct from dairy farms, and even then it has lost some flavour thanks to modern extraction methods: naturally skimmed cream is made by skimming off the cream that rises to the surface of the milk after 12 hours, and has a good full flavour. Single (light) cream has an 18 per cent fat content.

Sour cream – This is mostly used in savoury dishes rather than in desserts, but it may occasionally be called for in a sweet recipe.

Whipping cream – This is manufactured especially for whipping. All cream whips best at a cool temperature, between 5°C–10°C/ 40°F–50°F. If used straight from the refrigerator, it will not foam as much, and if it is too warm, it will be difficult to whip. Whipping cream cannot be boiled, and it has a fat content of 35 per cent.

Non-dairy alternatives – The ones I have tried are very good substitutes indeed and I wouldn't hesitate to use the single (light) or double (heavy) cream alternatives. Often the fat content is not much different to the real thing, and therefore they can be used for everything that double (heavy) or single (light) cream would be, including serving separately at the table. However, the keeping qualities are much improved – they will keep for about 3 or 4 weeks in the refrigerator. They have less flavour than real cream, though.

Sugar

Forty per cent of the world's sugar now comes from sugar beet rather than the sugar cane that was once the only source of sugar.

Caster (superfine) sugar – This is the most popular kind for use in baking, as it dissolves easily. The name comes from the sugar caster that was placed on the table, as it was usually filled with this sugar.

Demerara sugar – This has slightly larger crystals than light brown soft sugar and a more treacly flavour.

Granulated sugar – This is the type that I use for sugar syrup, as it is cheap but of good quality.

Icing (confectioners') sugar – This is a finely powdered form of sugar, particularly useful for decoration.

Muscovado sugar, dark – This has around a 13 per cent molasses content with a rich flavour. It has a fine-grained texture suitable for dark fruit cakes and puddings.

Muscovado sugar, light – This is an unrefined light brown soft sugar, with naturally present molasses and flavour – good for sticky puddings and cakes. It has a fine-grained texture.

Soft brown sugar, dark – This is sometimes known as Barbados sugar. It is a darker form of light brown soft sugar.

Soft brown sugar, light – This is usually a white sugar with a certain amount of cane molasses added for colour.

FROMAGE FRAIS

Natural fromage frais is a very fresh, soft and mildly flavoured cheese, which is usually used as an accompaniment, either as it is or with sieved icing (confectioners') sugar stirred in to it. Low-fat versions are available for those who prefer them. It is suitable for use in most dessert recipes, whether hot or cold, and is particularly useful as an ingredient in an accompanying cream or sauce. A quick dessert can be created using sweetened natural fromage frais mixed with the fruit purée of your choice.

MASCARPONE

This is a full-fat soft Italian cheese, served either as an accompaniment or in baked and cold dishes. Its creamy texture makes it a useful and versatile ingredient, and its subtle flavour complements most other ingredients well.

MILK

In all these recipes, skimmed or semi-skimmed milk can be substituted for full-fat milk if you are watching your fat intake.

Condensed milk continues to be popular – try making custard or crème anglaise using half condensed milk and half fresh milk. The sugar makes it ideal for *lait confiture*, as the French call the caramelizing process used in Banoffi Pie (see page 44).

INDEX